TURN THE OTHER CHEEK

A Story of Courage and Perseverance

Dorothy Annette Grant

Nov. 2

Dear Jody!

We must get together as I've heard wonderful things about you!

Dorothy Grant

 FriesenPress

Suite 300 - 990 Fort St
Victoria, BC, v8v 3K2
Canada

www.friesenpress.com

Copyright © 2016 by Dorothy Annette Grant
First Edition — 2016

All rights reserved.

No part of this publication may be reproduced in any form, or by any means, electronic or mechanical, including photocopying, recording, or any information browsing, storage, or retrieval system, without permission in writing from FriesenPress.

ISBN
978-1-4602-8947-1 (Hardcover)
978-1-4602-8948-8 (Paperback)
978-1-4602-8949-5 (eBook)

1. BIOGRAPHY & AUTOBIOGRAPHY

Distributed to the trade by The Ingram Book Company

TABLE OF CONTENTS

Forward...v

Chapter One
A Rude Awakening...1

Chapter Two
School Days..5

Chapter Three
Green Bay Summers..7

Chapter Four
A Slow and Painful Passing..9

Chapter Five
Theatrical Beginnings..11

Chapter Six
Friends, Foes and Follies at Mills Brothers...........................13

Chapter Seven
The Halifax Concert Parties..17

Chapter Eight
Voyage Overseas 25

Chapter Nine
The Tour Begins 31

Chapter Ten
Feeling at Home in London 35

Chapter Eleven
Across the Channel to Europe 37

Chapter Twelve –
A Horrifying Visit to Belsen 43

Chapter Thirteen
The Last Leg of the Overseas Tour 47

Chapter Fourteen
In the Hands of a Master Surgeon 51

Chapter Fifteen
McIndoe and His Amazing Guinea Pigs 59

Chapter Sixteen
Returning Home 63

Chapter Seventeen
Settling into Postwar Life 65

Chapter Eighteen
A Dramatic Change in Charlotte's Life 71

Chapter Nineteen
Charlotte Predictably Remains a Remarkable Woman 77

Epilogue 81

FORWARD

In 1974, while I was working as a freelance reporter in Halifax, I warned radio listeners in the city about a company that was scamming many local consumers.

After my damning report made the news, I found myself working for the CBC's television and radio stations in Halifax. I was soon covering many disturbing **consumer**-related issues and I often was able to help many people get the satisfaction they deserved.

In 1997, while I was on the staff of the Nova Scotia Medical Society, I received a letter from a lady named Charlotte Jefferies, who lives in Halifax. She contacted me at the Society to tell me that she knew that while I was at the CBC, I had been doing good things for people.

She explained that, in 1946, she had had plastic surgery performed by Sir Archibald McIndoe, a famous plastic surgeon in England, and when discharged had been given her medical records, which contained details of the surgery he had performed. She said this information was "a very important private and personal part of my life."

It seems, she had been seeing a Halifax plastic surgeon and had loaned him her charts. The surgeon had died and his secretary refused to return her charts.

It didn't take very long for me to "enlighten" this secretary that after more than ten years, Charlotte was entitled to her medical records, especially as they were the original copies that she had been given and she now legally owned.

When she received her charts she was very grateful. and I decided to meet Charlotte Jeffries in person. Almost immediately, I discovered that she is a woman with an awe-inspiring life story, that I want to share with you.

CHAPTER ONE
A RUDE AWAKENING

She was only five years old when it happened, but it is a memory that has never faded. As she lay pretending to sleep, Charlotte Jeffries heard the door to her room slowly opening and, through half-closed eyes, saw a thin slice of light invade the darkness. Her parents tiptoed to her bedside, and treading cautiously behind them was a very tall man. Standing side by side, the three people gazed intently at the little girl whom they thought was sound asleep. Charlotte immediately sensed that the man, whom she did not know, seemed to be focusing his attention on her face. Obviously disturbed by what he saw, he murmured, "Don't ever let her know that nothing can be done to help her."

Charlotte Guy was born in Halifax, Nova Scotia on May 13, 1921. Her father, George Guy, was a Haligonian and the assistant manager at the Royal Bank's main branch in the city. Her mother, Jeanne, was born in Truro, but had moved to Halifax as a young woman. The two were destined to marry. Little is known about their courtship, but it is likely they met while Jeanne was also an employee at the same Royal Bank.

When Charlotte was born, Jeanne and Guy had already been blessed with two sons—Thomas, age four, and Ross, two years old at the time. (Their first child, a daughter named Carrie Elizabeth, had died when she was only nine months old. The cause of her death is unknown.)

From the moment of their second daughter's birth, the couple faced a reality that all parents dread. They had to come to terms with the fact that their new baby's appearance was far from normal. Minutes after their family doctor delivered the newborn, he had to inform the new parents that their daughter had been born with a prominent congenital pigmented capillary cavernous haemagioma—commonly known as a port wine stain—on the right side of her face. It is now known that this facial anomaly occurs more often in females.

This type of facial disfigurement is significant and, predictably, would make most people feel uncomfortable expressing the standard clichés that are typically offered at the sight of a tiny infant. Saying, ""Isn't she adorable," unfortunately, would seem inappropriate, or insincere.

It is impossible to know how this devastating situation affected Jeanne and George Guy, but we do know that they were doting parents who never openly expressed any frustration or, it seems, angrily asked the predictable question, "Why did this happen to us and our beloved daughter?" Instead, the Guys focused their attention on searching for medical or surgical therapies that would improve their daughter's appearance. This became even more important as the years passed and Charlotte's facial anomalies became much more pronounced.

When Charlotte was a little girl you could see the birth defect on her face.

Charlotte now knows that when she was still very young, her parents travelled with her to see a doctor in Pittsburgh. Nothing positive came out of the appointment and she was never told anything about what they had learned during that costly trip to the US. She has since discovered that the physician who saw her in Pittsburgh was the same doctor who, a few years earlier, had whispered the shocking prognosis at her bedside.

Years after her parents' death, Charlotte speaks of her parents with great love in her voice. But she remains perplexed that she cannot recall them ever openly discussing her facial deformities with her. She views their reticence as bewildering because, as a young child, the stares she often experienced made it clear, that she was somehow very different from other girls her age. She regrets that her mother never raised the subject of her abnormal face, which had placed such an obvious strain on her early childhood. She believes an open discussion would have allowed her to share the awful anguish that she felt, but kept hidden inside herself.

Although they never spoke openly with her about her facial disfigurement, Charlotte's parents continued to search for therapies that might be beneficial. "I think I was only eleven or twelve when they began taking me to the Victoria General Hospital in Halifax for radium treatments," Charlotte recalls. "Each time I went there; a doctor would place what I now know was a small piece of lead-covered radium close to my lips. I was told that I had to sit perfectly still on a very uncomfortable wooden chair for at least twenty minutes. It was very frightening because I was left all alone in a gloomy x-ray room. I'm sure any little child in this kind of hostile setting would have felt as I did—totally abandoned."

It has been a long time since Charlotte had to endure those treatments, but the fear and the suffering she experienced remain a disturbing memory. "I'll never forget the strange smell that seemed to surround my face while I was being subjected to that therapy."

She has learned from specialists who have since treated her that those archaic treatments actually exacerbated her problem. "Sometimes, after the radium therapy, I would suddenly experience a lot of bleeding on the roof of my mouth," she says. "My poor father was very upset when this happened and he would take me to see our family doctor. The doctor would have me lie on a table with my head hanging down off of it. Then he would cauterize the bleeding area. The treatment was very painful."

Charlotte manages to smile a little when she speculates on how her two older brothers must have felt about their "strange"-looking little sister. "I'm sure they must have been embarrassed by my appearance, but I was a bit of a tomboy and really liked playing with my brothers and their friends," she says. "I suspect those other boys must have asked my brothers what was wrong with me. If they did, this was never shared with me. As far as I was concerned, Ross and Tom treated me the same way most brothers treat their younger sisters."

CHAPTER TWO
SCHOOL DAYS

When it came time for Charlotte to go to school, her father felt she should go to a public school. Her mother was completely opposed to doing this, probably because she feared her daughter would be subjected to ridicule in that kind of environment. She insisted that Charlotte be enrolled in a private girls' school, the Halifax Ladies College (now known as Armbrae Academy).

As it turned out, Jeanne Guy's instincts were spot on. Charlotte insists that during the twelve years she spent at the school, she never had to endure cruel remarks, and was never made to feel ashamed of her appearance.

Fortunately, Charlotte's childhood was generally a happy time in her life. She loved attending the Halifax Ladies College, where her unusual appearance was never mentioned, or was at least, sensitively ignored. She soon became known as one of the school's most enthusiastic students and athletes. Among her classmates was Budge Wilson, who grew up to become a well-known and most beloved Canadian author.

Looking back at those years, Charlotte is no longer reluctant to discuss the fact that dating, or teenage romances, were never possible or even contemplated. "I think I simply chose to avoid situations where this might have seemed important," she says.

Apparently, she had once confided to a friend, that she hoped, some day, she would find a blind man who would want to marry her.

She discloses that her coping methods became more essential as her facial disfigurement worsened. As she explains, "The redness on the right side of my face continued to spread and my nose became quite bulbous."

When Charlotte was fourteen, her parents arranged to have a family photograph taken. It was extremely unpleasant for her and she despised the results. "I hated that picture even though it was the only one ever taken of our family. Soon after I left home, I was delighted when I was able to tear it into very small pieces."

Only once did she actually "date" a young man. "He was a neighbour's son who took me to my high school graduation dance," recounts Charlotte. "I suppose his parents must have asked him to do this… there certainly wasn't anything romantic about that evening."

When Charlotte graduated in 1937, her class's yearbook had this to say about her:

> "Charlotte has been with us since kindergarten. This year she is a special student. We don't know what the school would do without her. Charlotte has been an energetic and skilful hockey and basketball player since the 2nd collegiate. She has an excellent ear for music and is also able to draw. She actually teaches art to two small boys. Next year, Charlotte will probably continue with her art and music."

Early in her life, it became obvious that Charlotte possessed a natural flair for music. "My parents told me that when I was only three or four I would go to the piano and pick out tunes," she says. Apparently, one day she astonished her parents by using one finger to play a few notes of Schubert's "Unfinished Symphony." As she explains, "I think I had heard it being played on our radio."

Recognizing she possessed outstanding musical talent, her parents arranged for her to take piano lessons. "My teacher's name was Ada Hoyt. She was just a wisp of a lady with very thick glasses," Charlotte recalls. "I stayed with her until I was well into my teens and she was very pleased when I successfully passed the junior level exams set by the McGill Conservatory of Music. I now know I received distinction."

Charlotte also displayed exceptional artistic talent and, while at the Halifax Ladies College, took art lessons from a teacher, Edith Smith, who had studied with one of the Group of Seven. She dismisses suggestions that she could also have capitalized on her artistic ability, but acknowledges that eventually she did find an opportunity to put this talent to good use.

CHAPTER THREE
GREEN BAY SUMMERS

Summer vacations were always a pleasant time in Charlotte's life, especially as she spent August with her best friend, Barbara Schwartz, at a cozy cottage in Green Bay, Lunenburg County. Barbara's younger sister, Molly, and her friend Budge Wilson also loved the cottage.

Today, in correspondence with Charlotte, Budge reminded her that they had done a commendable job tolerating the younger" silly" girls they had had to be kind to!

It was at this treasured summer spot that Charlotte learned to play the accordion. Ironically, the instrument had been rented, not for Charlotte, but for another young woman. The piano accordion immediately intimidated its intended player, who wanted nothing to do with it. Charlotte didn't share her aversion and quickly mastered the borrowed instrument.

"It was a lot of fun for me to play that accordion, especially when a young fellow from the local community would join me on the banjo," she says. "We'd sit on an ocean beach near a blazing fire, serenading a really appreciative audience."

Later in life, it was her piano-accordion performances that would ultimately lead her to become a much sought after musician.

Charlotte discloses that around this time that she happened to read an article in *Reader's Digest about* a product called "Cover Mark" —a makeup formulated to disguise severe burns and other severe skin abnormalities.

For Charlotte, the makeup represented a possible way to hide her disfigurement and she immediately sent away for the cosmetic. Soon after it arrived, she began getting out of bed early on summer mornings to use it. "It wasn't easy to apply but, happily, people assured me it substantially covered the port wine stain on my face."

Since those days at Green Bay, Charlotte has relied on many different, very expensive cosmetics to cover her birthmark. Applying this essential makeup soon became a tedious lifelong process that requires more than an hour of her time every morning.

Charlotte says few people have the slightest idea how her everyday life has been affected by her facial anomalies. "For example, when I began putting the special makeup on my face every day, I could no longer go swimming, which was something I had been doing since I was three years old," she laments. "You see, I certainly couldn't dive into the water… even just getting my face wet, my makeup would come off. And, later, when I tried to compensate for not going swimming by playing tennis with my brothers, who were champion tennis players, I had to deal with another awkward situation. The left, unaffected side of my face would become bright red from the heat, while the right side covered with makeup never changed. Surely people will understand if, at times, I felt exasperated."

CHAPTER FOUR
A SLOW AND PAINFUL PASSING

Charlotte was still in her teens when she found herself dealing with another disturbing challenge. This time it was the tragic implications of her mother's deteriorating health. Only in her late thirties, Jeanne Guy was slowing dying. "Our family doctor told us it was the nerves controlling her muscles that were affected," Charlotte says. "We now know that she had multiple sclerosis."

The next nine years were a time of great anguish for the Guy family. As Jeanne Guy became bedridden, she had to be carried up and down the stairs by her husband. Eventually, she required twenty-four-hour care and Charlotte became her mother's primary caregiver.

One day, Charlotte entered her mother's bedroom to make the heartbreaking discovery that she had died. Charlotte did not attend her mother's funeral. She believes it would have been too painful for her to endure. Two years after the death of his first wife, George Guy married a woman who was only nine years older than his daughter, Charlotte.

The wedding took place soon after Charlotte's father retired from the Royal Bank and accepted a position as manager of the Waegwoltic, a popular, upscale boat club in the south end of Halifax. At the time, it was an elitist establishment—for example, the club denied membership to the Jewish community.

Charlotte and her brothers soon found themselves adjusting, not only to a new lady in their home but, within just a few years, to two new half-brothers, Roger and George.

Like most young stepdaughters, Charlotte never grew close to her stepmother. She did, however, continue to live for a number of years with her father and stepmother at the family's living quarters at the Waegwoltic.

She would be in her mid-twenties before she finally left home and moved into an apartment of her own. Her new home was located on Spring Garden Road, above

Mills Brothers, the store where she was destined to become one of the sales staff's most valued members.

CHAPTER FIVE
THEATRICAL BEGINNINGS

Charlotte can't recall how she became involved in the Theatre Arts Guild, which was located on College Street in Halifax at that time, but says it was probably her participation in this group that led to her being employed as a part-time salesgirl at Mills Brothers. She assumes this happened because the store's owner, Hugh Mills, often acted in the guild's productions and he had met her there.

She was fascinated to discover that one of Hugh's favourite activities, when he wasn't at his store, was playing lead roles in theatre guild productions and in a popular CBC Halifax radio series *The Gillans*, about a Nova Scotia farm family. He performed on the program for more than fifteen years. She also learned that he was known as "Uncle Mel," the host of a popular radio show for young people. She admits that she never dreamed she was destined to perform on it.

At first, Charlotte volunteered as a hat check girl at the theatre but, when someone learned that she had artistic skills that weren't being utilized, she was commandeered to help paint the large backdrops needed for theatrical productions. (Many years later, she was surprised to learn that one of the backdrops she had painted for a Theatre Arts Guild play was still being used at the Fleet Air base in Shearwater, Nova Scotia.)

One day, while she was working on a backdrop, she noticed a young woman sitting alone in the empty theatre's auditorium. "That's how I happened to meet Lila Treadwell. She also played the piano accordion and was providing background music for some of the productions." The two young women—who both loved the piano and the piano accordion—bonded immediately.

Lila continued to provide background music for Theatre Art Guild productions, but soon she and Charlotte began to appear regularly on Hugh Mills' *Uncle Mel's Junior Radio Stars* program. It was broadcast weekly on Halifax's CNHS station and quickly became a popular showcase for local youngsters to show off their musical talents.

Soon children as young as four who lived in the Halifax, Dartmouth and Bedford communities were thrilled to be able to appear on Uncle Mel's program. Charlotte chuckles when she admits that some of the child performers "weren't very good!" Nevertheless, every young person who "starred" on Uncle Mel's show never forgot the thrill of actually being heard live on a radio program. Charlotte realizes that her frequent appearances on the show must have helped make her and Lila's outstanding musical talents much better known. And, she recognizes that they must have played a major role in the two becoming popular performers in many of the concerts that were held in Halifax during the Second World War.

CHAPTER SIX
FRIENDS, FOES AND FOLLIES AT MILLS BROTHERS

It wasn't long before Charlotte began working full time at the Mills Brothers store. Her primary role as a salesgirl soon changed when she was given the responsibility of using her artistic skills to create more appealing sales counters and front window displays that were so eye catching, people passing by found it impossible not to stop for a moment to gaze at them. (For example, she orchestrated an animated Snow White and the Seven Dwarfs window display, that for many years, captivated the attention of passersby.) Hugh Mills and his brother Willet owned Mills Brothers, a stylish women's store on Spring Garden Road in Halifax. As it happened, Willett was always more than happy to fulfill the role of silent partner. He was a quiet, reticent man, who religiously avoided the stresses associated with the salesman's role and was perfectly content to work behind the scenes, astutely managing the company's finances.

Hugh's wife Jean was a member of the wealthy Shatford family of Hubbards, Nova Scotia. She was an artistic and refined lady known for her impeccable taste and ability to tactfully address her husband's occasional over exuberance.

Hugh and Willet's sister, Gertrude Mills, was a remarkable woman. A graduate of Dalhousie University's Law School, she organized the university's first women's hockey team. She would also become the first female editor of a prestigious American law encyclopedia.

Charlotte confides that Gertrude suffered from depression. This probably explains why, to avoid very stressful situations, she often served as Hugh Mill's secretary. Nevertheless, she was destined to become Charlotte's devoted ally. The young woman's facial problems clearly concerned Gertrude, leading to her playing a major role in a search for corrective plastic surgery to reduce their severity. All three members of the Mills family became very fond of Charlotte who, after his wife Jean's death, would travel with Hugh Mills on an exciting buying trip to Europe.

Although Charlotte's priorities at the store soon didn't afford her as many opportunities to serve Mill's customers, many were anxious to have her assistance. Some, in fact, made it clear they believed they deserved her famously cordial attention.

Today, she is reticent to share titillating accounts of the many wealthy customers who often shopped at Mills Brothers. But, with a little persuasion, she does disclose some entertaining snippets of the more memorable and sometimes rather "emotive" shoppers she encountered over her more than twenty-five years at the store.

With a smile on her face, she recalls the arrival of some of the more "challenging" shoppers, who invariably created considerable tension. One customer of South American heritage would enter the store with a dramatic flourish, clapping her hands loudly to capture everyone's attention. To the staff, this flamboyant salutation represented an ominous warning that sent many a saleslady fleeing to the washroom, or to a hiding place behind a counter.

Possessing the intimidating qualities of a movie star, this woman was such a demanding customer, and her shopping habits so capricious, she was viewed as a retail nightmare that the store's staff truly dreaded serving.

Another lady was a notorious shoplifter who, fortunately for her, had a very tolerant and wealthy husband. He appropriately responded to her illegal activities by setting up a charge account that could be accessed readily to pay for her "purchases."

One story Charlotte particular enjoys sharing is that of a wealthy husband who ritually, every Christmas, bought his wife lovely gifts such as luxurious lingerie. She is convinced the gifts must have made an impressive display under the family's Christmas tree but, predictably, only a few days after the end of the festive season, all of the gifts would be returned for a refund!

Another one of her most devoted shoppers turned out to be the city's most cosmopolitan Norwegian man, who was in charge of a Norwegian seamen's home. Charlotte had played there and he obviously liked to drop into Mills Brothers to see her. He soon presented her with a most debonair picture of himself taken at an exclusive photography studio in London, England. Charlotte still has some of the notes he sent to her, which express his deep affection and how anxious he was to have her play the piano for him. She shrugs when one comments on his urbane demeanor, and insists he was merely a smooth version of a Sir Galahad.

What Charlotte will never talk about is the fact that the left side of her face was quite beautiful and that she had a figure rivalling the legendary body of the movie star Esther Williams. Often dressed in lovely clothes she purchased from the Mills Brothers Store, in photographs she displays the striking body image of a fashion model. For her, however, these physical attributes could never compensate for the port wine stain that covered the right side of her face.

CHAPTER SEVEN
THE HALIFAX CONCERT PARTIES

Charlotte's life was dramatically altered in 1940, with the advent of the Second World War. The conflict thrust her into what was destined to become a true theatrical adventure. Barely in her twenties when war was declared, she was suddenly faced with the task of working all day at Mills Brothers, followed by long hours on evenings and weekends helping to entertain thousands of Canada's military personnel. To fully understand how Charlotte's life was so transformed, one must read an article entitled "The Halifax Concert Party in World War II," written by Professor Patrick O'Neil and published in the *Theatre Research Review* in the fall of 1999 (Vol.20.no.2).

O'Neil produced a definitive report on the concert parties. These began to thrive shortly after the outbreak of the war—on September 10, 1939—as civilian groups across Canada quickly organized and began offering their services to entertain the military mustering in Canada.

O'Neil learned that it was Hugh Mills who probably deserves the most credit for creating a dynamic entertainment program for the military stationed in Halifax. By early January 1940, Mills had assumed a daunting agenda strategically aimed at providing entertainment to boost the morale of soldiers, sailors, airmen and merchant marines arriving in Halifax. He somehow orchestrated this from a little office at the back of his Mills Brothers store. It was quickly transformed into the "command central" of what would soon become known as the Halifax Concert Parties Guild.

Remarkably, in this cramped setting as many as seven concert party shows were often organized in a single day. In fact, throughout the war, the Mills team—made up of Hugh Mills, his wife Jean and sister Gertrude—orchestrated up to fifteen shows in a single week. Complicating their endeavors was the fact that as many as twenty artists, from a long list of 700 candidates, had to be recruited to appear in each concert. Attendance at the shows varied from thirty-five to four thousand, depending on the location, but there was always a capacity crowd.

In a radio interview during the war, Hugh Mills recalled how diverse the settings could be: "It might be a lonely outpost where old mess tables are stuck together as an improvised stage and perhaps some of the boys hold on to it to see that the stage doesn't collapse under the feet of the tap dancers. Or, it might be from trucks in the open air!"

In addition to this huge contribution to the war effort, O'Neil reports that the Halifax Concert Parties Guild helped the military organize service personnel entertainment units. Supplies collected by the Guild, estimated to be worth millions of dollars, were made available to military outposts and ships of any allied nation. The donated items included curtains, costumes, furniture, radios, pianos, photographs, jigsaw puzzles, and so on. Many of the gifts were later lost at sea when merchant and navy ships carrying them were attacked by enemy submarines.

O'Neil was delighted to learn in 1996 that Charlotte was still a very active senior living in Halifax. He was even more encouraged to hear she had remarkable memories of the parties and he was quite anxious to interview her. To his delight, she was (and still is) able to provide intriguing recollections of the shows and the complicated logistics required to carry them off.

For example, Charlotte recalled that arranging a concert always required the Mills team to make dozens of phone calls to civilian and military performers who had told them that they were willing to participate in the performances (usually the shows took place after most of the entertainers had already spent a full day at their jobs).

The chosen performers represented a wonderful collection of talent since they included singers, dancers, yodelers, musicians, magicians, actors, radio personalities, opera stars—all of them ready, at a moment's notice, to perform anywhere and everywhere, from churches and halls to social clubs, military bases, ships, hospitals and even on trains. Also on their roster were the yet-to-be-famous performers, such as Gordie Tapp and Murray Westgate. At the time, Tapp was a soldier in the Canadian Army and Westgate a signalman in the navy.

Charlotte says she first met Murray Westgate during her Sunday piano performances at a church hall that hosted servicemen. She speaks fondly of him and how he would often walk her home to her nearby residence. She still has a number of pictures he gave or sent to her. Best of all, Murray and Gordie became Charlotte's lifelong friends and continued to visit and contact her long after the war years had ended. Westgate is now more than 95 years old, lives in a veterans" facility in Toronto. What is so remarkable in Charlotte's case is that her appearances at the concerts required her to get up out of bed at least an hour before everyone else to apply the makeup that concealed her facial deformities. It is important to note that in most of the pictures that were taken of her, she posed with the unaffected left side of her face toward the camera.

Having performed as an accompanist with the group over a thousand times, Charlotte still vividly remembers those evening jaunts and she shared the episodes with O'Neil: "Every night we would be off to one of these concerts and we'd get to the most unusual places." These out-of-the-way places included the *Sir James Ross,* a Norwegian whaling ship, the *Pasteur,* a free French battleship, and the *Lady Nelson,* a Canadian hospital ship. She also recalls the hazards they faced in the winter, which required her to climb out of a motor launch and up an ice-covered ladder while wearing an evening gown and high heels.

Charlotte and Lila entertain "happy" Swedish sailors during Second World War on Shore Leave in Halifax.

Other times, Charlotte and various performers piled into the two station wagons maintained by the group or into borrowed army trucks for a long drive to some more remote military installation or coastal battery—York Redoubt, H.M.C.S.

Dockyard, Fort Ogilvie, Sandwich Battery, Camp Hill Hospital, Camp Aldershot. Not to be forgotten was a visit to the Cornwallis Naval Base in Deep brook, Nova Scotia, where, after they had finished a performance, two thousand naval recruits threw their caps high into the air to show their appreciation.

Charlotte candidly admits that while all this may sound like a lot of fun, it represented enormous challenges for the Mills family and its courageous performers. She still laughs when asked to describe her wartime adventures, "We never went to the air base at Stanley, just outside of Truro, without getting lost!"

She also told O'Neil about a scary event one evening when they were returning from York Redoubt, near Halifax. It was pitch black and the road was icy when they came upon a convoy travelling out of Halifax and their station wagon suddenly spun out of control. She admitted she was terrified and felt certain that they would end up on the bottom of the Northwest Arm.

Charlotte still treasures the autographed program she received at a guild performance on December 1, 1941, at the Capitol Theatre in Halifax, when Gracie Fields was the star attraction. The Navy League of Canada was sponsoring Gracie, billed as "The Empire's Most Popular Artist." Those who attended that night's performance were told that, for fifty cents, they could purchase an autographed photo of Gracie. They were also advised that the entire proceeds of the sale of her pictures "will be devoted to the maintenance of the Gracie Field's Orphanage in England." Charlotte was thrilled to meet Gracie on this special evening.

This picture of Lila *and Charlotte was featured for many years on one of the walls at the Capital Theatre.*

A year later, during the summer of 1942, Charlotte met Babe Ruth when he was the guest of honor at the Wanderers' Ball Park in Halifax. The park had been spruced up to be re-commissioned as the recreation center for the Royal Canadian Navy. As the official opening approached—the date was set for August 1, 1942—the city hummed with rumors that Ruth would suit up and take part in a baseball game, even though it had been a number of years since he retired from the New York Yankees. While this momentous event didn't happen, Ruth did give a hitting exhibition for the five thousand fans that attended the game—dressed in smart street clothes. Afterwards, the crowd went wild when he tossed autographed baseballs to them.

Ruth, it seems, had significant personal links to Nova Scotia because of his great love of golf and fishing. These favourite pastimes, no doubt, influenced him to vacation in the province quite often, but the real reason was a man named Brother Matthias. Born in Lingan, Cape Breton, Matthias had been Ruth's baseball coach and a trusted mentor early in his career.

After the official opening of the ballpark, Ruth joined a number of entertainers, including Charlotte, at what was then a Y Depot where soldiers waiting to go overseas were billeted. His arrival was a great thrill for every one of them. Today, a picture of her with Babe Ruth and every other local entertainers is on Charlotte's kitchen wall.

This picture was taken at the Y Depot in Halifax. Babe Ruth is looking at a singer dressed in white next to him. **Hugh Mills is in front with a lady's hand on his shoulder, and Charlotte is at the far right wearing a striped skirt.**

Also among her memorabilia are pictures and mementos of Raymond Massey, the distinguished actor; John Fisher, who became known as Mr. Canada, J. Frank Willis, of Moose River fame, Portia White, the African–Nova Scotian contralto; and Max Ferguson, who was destined to become one of the CBC's favourite broadcasters. During the war years, all of these luminaries crossed Charlotte's path.

It is not possible for Charlotte to describe all of the many moving events she experienced during those years in which the Halifax Concert Party entertained the estimated half-million servicemen who passed through Halifax during the war (combined attendance at free band concerts and concert parties in what was known as Military District 6 has been estimated at 1.4 million).

Nevertheless, several events do stand out. One of them happened when the hospital ship *Letitia* docked in Halifax. What followed set a precedent because, for the first time, civilian entertainers were allowed to play at the dockside for the wounded men arriving in the city from the Front. In the past it was usually a service band that provided this diversion, as casualties were brought to shore. On this memorable occasion, piano accordionists Charlotte Guy and Lila Treadwell, along with singer Betty Jean Ferguson (who would later become Miss Canada 1948). The Halifax Symphony's concert master, violinist, Julius Silverman, also performed. After entertaining the ship's passengers at the dockside, the four moved on to the hospital train. There they performed for three and a half hours, going from one car to another as the wounded men they passed yelled for more.

Another similar event generated great admiration for members of the Halifax Concert Party Guild. This outstanding occasion was noted in a *Halifax Herald* headline, which read "Musical Cheer Hospital Train." In this case, Lila and Charlotte, who were described as some of Halifax's most talented musicians, joined a contralto named Dorothy Hamilton to meet the *Lady Nelson* at the pier where it had docked, at the request of the Red Cross.

After their dockside performance, the three women boarded the hospital train, which was waiting nearby to transport wounded soldiers to their homes across Canada. Soon, the musicians were weaving their way through the train, crowded with hundreds of war-weary passengers. One of the Red Cross workers was awed by the way their music lifted the spirits of the wounded men.

A nurse waiting in the last car with four severely wounded and depressed men felt there was little hope they would enjoy the entertainment. To her delight, when Charlotte and Lila came through playing their accordions, with Dorothy and all of them singing, every one of her patients began to smile! It was a touching scene. Later, as the train left the station, the trio of troubadours continued to serenade the men from the platform, to the loud applause of convalescent soldiers hanging out the train windows.

For Charlotte, the Second World War would represent one of the most fulfilling periods in her life. It would also soon result in her becoming part of a group of musicians who would bring heartening entertainment to thousands of Canadian troops and survivors of the war in Europe.

CHAPTER EIGHT
VOYAGE OVERSEAS

It was after a Halifax Concert Party performance on the hospital ship *Lady Nelson* that the idea of taking the show overseas was first raised. It seems some of the ship's officers were enjoying a few drinks with Hugh Mills when Mills mentioned he would like to take some members of his company to Europe.

Mills must have been delighted when the officers responded by telling him they had lots of room on their ship and, since they were bound for England, suggested the Halifax Concert Party members could come along and entertain the wounded servicemen heading home.

Mills must have been delighted with their offer but wisely realized he would have to jump through a number of military "hoops" to secure the necessary permissions. With this objective in mind, he wrote to the Adjutant General in Ottawa in August 1944. As he pointed out to the adjutant, the Halifax Concert Party had given more performances than any other such group in Canada. He also indicated that, along with himself and his wife Jean, the group of entertainers to voyage overseas would be small—ten women and only one man. And, most importantly, his proposal wouldn't cost the government a single penny.

Almost immediately, he received a negative response to his proposal. It arrived in a letter from a Captain William Fields of the Auxiliary Services (Army) which read: "To permit you to send a concert party abroad would open the floodgates to every other civilian group in Canada that might want to do the same thing."

It's not known what eventually transpired to overcome this discouraging rejection, but Charlotte certainly recalls the day Hugh Mills announced that she and nine other female members of the Halifax Concert Party group, along with Halifax Symphony violinist Julius Silverman, as well as Mills and his wife, were going to Europe.

Charlotte initially decided she couldn't go with them. "Every morning I always had to get up early to apply my makeup. Naturally, I never wanted people to see me without it. So, the thought of going overseas into a situation where I would lose my privacy, I just couldn't deal with. But somehow, it was arranged that I'd always share my accommodation with Irene Spence, one of my best friends, and this convinced me to go on the tour overseas."

While Charlotte knew very little about the reasons behind the decision to allow the Halifax Concert Party members to go to Europe, she quickly became aware that the military had issued a number of rules specifically for them. She still has a copy of these rules, which prohibited them from attending entertainments, dances or parties, and imposed a curfew of 2300 hours. Most significantly, they were ordered to follow all army directives, which would create intriguing and rather intimidating military regulations for these young civilians.

Charlotte says they realized they were about to assume a very responsible role, "We were immediately designated temporary active members of the army and learned we were receiving financial support from the *Halifax Herald* newspaper. I'll never forget one day going to the Cogswell Street Military Hospital in the north end of Halifax where we all got three inoculations in each of our arms."

According to her, the event was very trying, "We played for a few hours and poor Julius later complained of a very painful arm but I didn't experience any discomfort—maybe because of the exercise I received from playing my piano accordion.

Charlotte and Lila playing their musical instruments with Julius accompanying them on his violin. They often appeared as a trio.

Within days of receiving the overseas permission, the ten women found themselves outfitted with uniforms resembling members of the CWAC (Canadian Women's Army Corp). This included full battle dress; Charlotte still has her black army boots. The patch on their uniforms read: Civilian Concert Party Canada. Julius wore the same army uniform. The only difference in their attire was that their buttons were made of leather, not brass, and they were given maroon, not black, berets. As it turned out, wearing this kind of uniform would be a huge asset for the women when they were, at last, overseas.

July 19, 1945, was the fateful day the group, now billed as the Halifax Herald Concert Party, boarded the *Ile de France*, which was bound for England. Their role had been clearly defined—they were to entertain troops in Europe during long delays in repatriation—and they were destined to do this in an outstanding way.

Charlotte kept a diary of the ocean voyage, which she faithfully recorded at the end of each day at sea. The very first night, she wrote about a visit they had received from Abbie Lane, then the mayor of Halifax, and added the news that, "the ship did not sail as scheduled due to a naval explosion." The explosion, at a munitions depot in the Bedford Basin, triggered intense fear among the general population. In fact, the next day the *Toronto Star* newspaper reported that 15,000 people from Halifax and 10,000 from Dartmouth had been evacuated from their homes.

Charlotte, who had learned long ago how to cope with challenging situations, merely wrote in her diary, "We drifted back to sleep only to be awakened at ten to four by a terrific blast. We again drifted back to sleep."

During the days that followed on the *Ile de France*, Charlotte and her fellow entertainers performed a number of times for the passengers and crew. Among the people on board were the members of an army pipe band, New Zealand and Canadian air force officers, members of the Canadian Women's Army Corps and refugee children going home.

One of the more unforgettable moments for Charlotte, who was slowly adapting to the Atlantic's fickle ways, was "going down into the hold to put on my costumes for an evening show… boy, did it feel queer down there," she wrote. "I can now say that I was down in the bowels of the *Ile de France*."

She also wrote that one evening, as she, Lila and Julius did "a tour around all of the decks," playing their instruments, the British guest children on board joined in and sang songs.

There is little doubt, however, that one of the most moving moments of her ocean journey transpired on July 22, during a Protestant church service in the officers' lounge. She and Lila, as usual, performed on their piano accordions, joined by Julius on the violin, and the music they presented created an almost spiritual-like atmosphere.

Hugh's wife, Jean, had also begun to chronicle their voyage to Europe and send her reports to the *Halifax Herald*, which had funded the concert party's overseas initiative. In her first letter to the newspaper, using her pen name "Aunt Mel," Jean disclosed that on the group's first day aboard the *Ile de France*, a meeting was held to discuss entertainment for the troops and other passengers during the five-or-six-day crossing.

"From then on things began to hum," she wrote. "One of the commandant's chief concerns was to get some things going to keep the British war guest children occupied. As there were over a hundred of them, of course, it was a desirable thing to consider."

Apparently, this duty fell into Hugh Mills' hands and, before long, an audition was organized. A number of children, a few rather reluctantly, lined up and marched around the deck singing, "*I'm Going to take a Sentimental Journey*" and "*Wish me Good Luck as You Wave me Goodbye*," accompanied by Charlotte and Lila on the accordions and Julius on violin. One little girl, whom they discovered was from Millsboro, England, possessed a clear and melodious singing voice. "The audience cheered and applauded to such an extent she almost stopped the show. Everyone said that they were sure that she would be heard from in the future," wrote Aunt Mel in her first letter to the *Halifax Herald*.

Aunt Mel also shared some of the most stirring moments of that church service, noting that more than 400 people attended. "The choir was made up of the girls of the concert party on one side and men of the air force on the other. As we looked down from the balcony and saw all of the members of the Canadian Women's Army Corps with their brass glittering, the Navy standing at attention, and the British War guests looking very seriously at our improvised church alter, we again forgot that we were on board a ship."

She spoke of how reassuring it was to recognize that those attending the event were clearly captivated by Julius the violinist who, with Charlotte and Lila playing their piano accordions, performed the hymns, "*Ava Maria*" and "*The Rosary*."

Equally inspiring for the audience, she wrote, was the poignant rendition of the *Lord's Prayer* sung by contralto Dorothy Hamilton (She would perform this Christian hymn a number of times during their time in Europe).

Shortly after the service, Aunt Mel shared the excitement everyone was feeling about soon being able to lay their eyes on the coast of Ireland: "Many eyes were scanning the horizon for just a glimpse of the Emerald Isles." When they finally saw the island, Charlotte and Lila and Julius celebrated by playing Irish airs. Not surprisingly, there were very few who weren't on deck to observe the view. "Later, sailing up the Clyde was one of the most beautiful sights we had ever seen," wrote Aunt Mel. "Any Scottish heart would have been moved had they heard the CWAC pipe band piping us up the river."

The next morning the group boarded a tender that was to take them to the pier at Gourock, Scotland. Due to a delay with the train, they were once again asked to give a brief performance—this time, their first on Scottish soil!

CHAPTER NINE
THE TOUR BEGINS

The next day the group found themselves in Aldershot, today known as the Home of the British Army. When "The Halifax Heralds," as they became known, arrived there in July, 1945, they were sent directly to a building run by the Canadian Legion. It turned out to be a comfortable, welcoming place and the group was soon made to feel right at home.

They were all aware that, although they weren't in the regular Canadian army, they had been instructed to follow all of its directives. To assist them in achieving this, they were assigned an army sergeant who did his level best to turn them into an acceptable version of the "real thing."

This intimidating-looking soldier immediately proceeded to deliver a string of military orders, but Charlotte laughs when she recalls his attempt to get them to parade as new troops. It was a dismal failure, in spite of the sergeant's efforts. "What he didn't know—or probably couldn't have cared less about—was that while we could perform beautifully on stage together, we just couldn't march in unison!" She might have smugly added that they could perform much better wearing high heels.

Soon the Halifax Heralds were performing for hundreds of Canadian soldiers waiting to be repatriated. Their first show took place early in the afternoon of August 7, 1945, at Witley Camp in Witley, England, and that evening at the Huron Camp, Bramshott. Their audience was Canadian soldiers waiting to be sent home to rest and recover.

They soon discovered that getting ready for their appearances was a challenge. They often had to crowd into small dressing rooms, which with their lack of elbow room made it very difficult to apply makeup and, as they reported, "make sure our costumes wouldn't accidentally fall off!" Nevertheless, the performers adapted, because they had learned that if the audiences were kept waiting too long, they would become restless. Wanting to start every show on the best possible note, they resolved to do their best to begin their performances on time.

They were surprised by how often they would find a large number of Maritimers waiting at the stage door for a word with the girls, full of eager questions like, "Are things just the same back home?" It pleased the Halifax Heralds enormously to know their appearances made so many hometown lads feel a little less far away from those they were so anxiously waiting to see again.

A key element in the performers' success was that the young women were in the same age group as most of the soldiers they were entertaining, and everywhere they went, they met former Halifax schoolmates, friends of families they knew, and even neighbours they had known before going overseas.

One of their most memorable concerts in England took place on August 10, 1945, at a hospital for Canadian soldiers in Taplow. The hospital was located in part of the Viscount and Lady Astor estate known as Clivedon. The 375-acre estate was graced with magnificent gardens and woodlands in Buckinghamshire on the River Thames. Lord Astor first ran a hospital for Canadian soldiers there during World War One, and then again during World War Two. It seems, however, that Lady Astor had openly expressed a preference for the veterans of the previous war.

The Halifax Herald's Clivedon performance was held in an auditorium on the lush grounds surrounding the expansive estate. Jean Mills disclosed, "We did our first show for walking patients or for those whose beds could be moved into the auditorium. After the stage show, a supervisor asked if we would mind visiting one or two wards."

In fact, thanks to the portability of the performers' instruments, Charlotte, Lila and Julius were able to give short concerts in fourteen wards.

Charlotte remembers those performances well. "One of the supervisors told us she was amazed at our stamina and noted that no previous concert party had ever presented so many shows in one day," she recalls.

Something interesting to note is that the Canadian Red Cross had donated high-grade apples from Nova Scotia to many army, navy and air force hospitals during the war. The Red Cross hospital at Taplow also received this delicious gift of Nova Scotia's apples.

None of the Halifax Herald group ever did catch sight of the Astors. Perhaps this was because the nobles did not have a happy marriage. Lady Astor was an adherent of the Christian Scientist church and was most unsupportive of her husband's serious health problems.

Years, later, it is reported that Lady Astor had quarreled with her husband about, of all things, chocolate.

After performing at a number of military hospitals and bases, the group visited Leatherhead on August 15, 1945, Victory over Japan (V-J) Day. This town near Aldershot was well known and highly regarded for its hospitality to the Canadian military. The Halifax Heralds had been asked to go there to give a concert for the townspeople.

At 10:30 p.m., their show began in the Crescent Theatre, "one of the most beautiful little theatres in which we ever played.

Charlotte can still visualize this unforgettable event, " The theatre sat 1,300 but counting those standing and children sitting on parents' laps, Jean Mills estimated the audience to number over 1,500. Their performance was a hit. At the end of the show, everyone joined hands and sang, "*Auld Lang Syne*," which they all agreed was very moving. They were all thrilled when the town's mayor gave a special thanks to Canada amidst the cheers of the thrilled local residents who had attended the joyous V-J Day celebration.

CHAPTER TEN
FEELING AT HOME IN LONDON

In a letter to the *Halifax Herald*, Jean Mills, a.k.a. Aunt Mel, describes this pleasant experience: "The first evening in London we decided to go to see Buckingham Palace… As we paraded through the streets, we were amazed at how much interest was shown in our girls… and it was not just because they were girls, either. It was that flash on their shoulders that read 'Canada.'"

It seems the group was particularly attractive to Canadian servicemen, who were not shy to stop them on the street. Jean Mills describes that which followed, "they would come up to us, and say, 'What part of Canada does this outfit come from?' or 'Fellows, listen to that good old Canadian lingo!' Questions were put to us by the score and, when we would start to move on, they would say, 'Hey, just a few more words for us.'" The members of the group were gratified to discover how much their arrival meant to the Canadian servicemen they met who were so glad they had made the journey overseas.

Charlotte says she had quickly recognized why they were receiving so much attention from the Canadian soldiers and civilians they encountered. "People on the streets in London thought we were Canadian female paratroopers!" As it turns out, people drew this conclusion from the maroon berets that graced the performers' heads—headwear that was typically seen only on Canadian male paratroopers.

At the end of their first long day in London—which included a visit to St. Paul's Cathedral and a steep climb up the 627 steps to its tower—Jean Mills said the girls were ready to head home. They were relieved to find a place that felt like the closest thing to home—accommodations at the Canadian YWCA.

The women were delighted to discover that the YWCA's dietitian was one Mrs. Gerry Chambers, a native of Truro, Nova Scotia. They were further reassured to learn that each dormitory in the building was named after one of Canada's provinces and that, over each bed, the name of one of the towns or cities of that province was printed in bright colours. Jean Mills insisted, "The girls will never forget London, or the YWCA where they were so warmly welcomed."

CHAPTER ELEVEN
ACROSS THE CHANNEL TO EUROPE

The Halifax Heralds set foot on the soil of Continental Europe on August 29 - their first steps of what would prove to be a 6,300-mile tour through Belgium, the Netherlands and Germany. According to Patrick O'Neil, the group consisted of the ten concert party members and Julius, the Mills, twelve stagehands (one of whom was Brett Fader, a Halifax man in charge of their sound requirements) and a liaison officer.

No doubt there must have been some apprehension among the musicians, singers and dancers, but they soon discovered their performances were always greeted with enthusiasm by grateful audiences in packed houses.

It's important to disclose how the Halifax Herald Concert Party members would be transported in the demanding weeks ahead. There was a bus for the artists—a modified dental wagon—and there was also a heavy utility personnel vehicle and two other trucks, plus a sixty-ton transport truck to carry two pianos, scenery, musical instruments, fixtures and costumes. Also among their equipment was a generating plant for providing complete stage lighting, since it was essential this be available if other sources failed, or weren't available at a concert site.

The Halifax Heralds in front of the modified dental truck that transported them around Europe. Charlotte is at the right end of the group.

The party had been told originally that their first European destination would be Holland, but instead they were rather disappointed to learn it would be Germany. On their way to that country, they made a brief stop in Ghent, Belgium, for a snack, and then began a long, slow drive through war-torn Holland. As they were passing through Holland, they were surprised to discover the inhabitants were celebrating their queen's birthday.

The Canadians were amazed to find the towns and villages decorated with a profusion of flowers, and delighted in passing through archways of heather entwined with orange flowers. Every little girl had an orange ribbon in her hair and the men and women wore flowers in their national colours. What they found most astounding, however, was that the people were celebrating amidst the shattered ruins of bombed-out buildings. They would have loved to stop and spend some time in this remarkably resilient country, but their destination was Aurick, on the windswept flats of northwest Germany.

If the young Nova Scotian entertainers had harbored any reticence about this engagement, it was soon washed away. As Jean Mills reported, "They walked right into the hearts of the Canadian troops" who were occupying the little town. After the show was over, a few of the Halifax Heralds stayed in the theatre to watch the audience depart and to greet anyone from home. They soon noticed an old German man and woman going carefully along each aisle "butt snipping." This involved picking up every single cigarette butt and placing it into a black bag. They learned that these people would take the butts home, remove the paper and use the tobacco to trade for food.

As temporary members of the Canadian Army, each of the Halifax Heralds received an allotment of 900 cigarettes a month. Since most of the performers were non-smokers and failed to recognize the importance of this allotment, they soon began making presents of these cigarettes to people they met. Charlotte admits some of them couldn't resist trading a few cigarettes for little souvenirs of the countries they were visiting.

In Aurick, the group witnessed the disheartening effects of the war on survivors' lives. The women were dressed in shabby clothing, with unkempt hair and faces bare of any makeup. It was pitiful to see them go with their shopping bags to find what they could in almost-empty shops. Wounded German citizens were often on the streets they drove through and it was hard for the Canadians to disregard the expressions on people's faces, which seemed to say , "Look what you did to us."

Later, when they were billeted in Wilhelmshaven, in what used to be a German naval barracks, the Halifax Heralds felt surrounded by an atmosphere of unfriendliness and unhappiness. Although the Germans were polite and courteous, whenever the Heralds happened to approach them, they sensed a definite hostility.

Charlotte is almost apologetic when she admits that she could truly understand their reaction. "It was stressed that we shouldn't show any kindness to the Germans and we were told not to speak to them and we were also informed that when we passed Germans on the street, they were expected to step aside for us," Charlotte recalls, "We kind of ignored these instructions, because it wasn't our nature to be like this."

Nevertheless, no one could have prepared the young Nova Scotians for the extreme tension the war had created between the Germans and the Canadian Occupying Forces. This harsh reality was dramatically conveyed to them when they toured Wilhelmshaven's harbour and saw the anger and hostility in the eyes of former sailors, that they would dare display a sense of pride as they were shown the ruins of sunken German ships.

Jean Mills spoke about the obvious resentment they were experiencing in a September letter to the *Herald*: "Little did we realize back home how much the occupational forces here in Germany are going through. Here they are in a hostile country where it is at least unwise to be friendly and where one's natural impulses have to be quelled. It does display something that cannot be explained and although there are many times when we are lonely, too, we feel very thankful that we are here doing something to help while away the odd tedious evening."

Next, they visited the small town of Varel, where they stayed at the 2nd Canadian Legion Hotel and were surprised and delighted to find that its supervisor was a man from Halifax.

Jean Mills wrote, "It is difficult to explain the wonderful reaction… when we meet Nova Scotians in Germany. It tends to lighten the gloom that hangs heavily here. Nevertheless, being around so many people who clearly found it hard to hide their anger for having been so badly defeated, was very disheartening for the Halifax Heralds."

The Canadian military soon became aware of the effect of the tour on the performers' morale and wisely decided to limit their stay in Germany to two weeks. In mid-September, they left Germany and travelled to Groningen, Netherlands.

Returning to Holland immediately lifted the Halifax Heralds' collective spirits. Jean Mills wrote about their feelings in one of her letters to the *Halifax Herald*: "I don't think we will ever find words to describe the feeling of relief when we crossed the border into Holland… we were so relieved because we were greeted as if we were liberators."

Jean admits they nearly fell out of the windows of their vehicles, waving to people and throwing candy to children who ran out of their homes to greet them. She adds, "The 'clip clop' of their wooden shoes was music to our ears."

The highlight of their first week in Holland was a visit to Akkrum, where Halifax's own Princess Louise Fusiliers were stationed. Once again, the concert group represented the most fitting way to repay the city's residents for the kindness they had shown to Canadian soldiers. They were delighted to do this and gave a performance in a large factory.

Charlotte still recalls being impressed when, after their show was over, she and all of the cast members were each presented with a beautiful bouquet of flowers. And just as unforgettable was riding in their flower-laden bus as it inched its way through the crowded street near the factory where they had entertained. As they passed, the people of Akkrum loudly cheered them on, not just for the wonderful concert but also to show their lasting gratitude for the pivotal role Canada had played in the liberation of Holland.

By this point in their European tour, the Halifax Heralds had believed they would be returning to Canada, but this didn't happen. They had just completed a week's run from October 15 to 20 at the Tuschinski Theatre in Amsterdam, which Charlotte remembers as one of the world's most beautiful theatres. To their great surprise, the Canadian Army asked the Halifax Heralds to extend their tour a little longer, and return to Germany for a short time.

The Halifax Herald's newspaper story of the women having their contract extended. On their way back to Germany, Charlotte and Mrs. Mills in front with flowers they had received from Canadian service men who had really appreciated their performances.

There is no information about how they reacted to this request, but we do know that after they had completed all of their performances in Amsterdam, the Heralds boarded their bus and headed to Schleswig, Germany, to perform for the 83rd Group Royal Air Force in the afternoon of October 23, and for the 406th Group Royal Canadian Air Force that evening. According to Charlotte, "We may have dreaded it, but the trip back to that country was not as unpleasant as we had imagined."

As they travelled through the German countryside to their next performance, the leaves were turning magnificent colours—just as in Canada in the late fall. They were soon re-invigorated by a triumphant performance in Schleswig, which proved to be a real boost for the group's morale.

Unfortunately, as they approached the next towns of Bremen, Kiel, and Hamburg, the beauty of the brightly coloured trees they had passed days before was erased from their minds as they saw these once-stately cities in total ruin.

Jean Mills in her November 13, 1945, letter to the *Herald* expressed how they had felt: "It is difficult to picture the absolute destruction of these cities. We wondered as we drove along if they could ever be built up again in our generation."

In Hamburg, they encountered a significant problem. Up until their arrival, only German Concert Parties had entertained the ship they were to visit, and so it was assumed they were German performers. In fact, when they appeared alongside a ship painted with the words "Allied Merchant Seaman Club," a first lieutenant curtly asked them, "Can you speak English?" When they told him they could and that they were, in fact, Canadian, everything changed and they were warmly welcomed aboard.

It was also in Hamburg that they were taken to a British officer's club for lunch. The club had once been the home of a German millionaire who had been too friendly with the Nazis and ended up in a concentration camp. It was a spectacular home with beautiful carved woodwork that truly impressed the group because all of it was made of Canadian maple.

CHAPTER TWELVE
A HORRIFYING VISIT TO BELSEN

Not long after their visit to Hamburg, the Halifax Heralds learned the RCAF station where they would be staying in Celle, Germany was only a half hour away from the Bergen-Belsen concentration camp (also known simply as Belsen). Information about concentration camps and the fates of prisoners was sparse in these days, so the Halifax Heralds were unaware of recent events involving the camp. They were naturally intrigued when they were told that they would be taken to Belsen for an inspection tour.

Unbeknownst to the Halifax Heralds, on April 8, 1945, the Allies had carried out their only serious bombing attack on Celle during the war, hitting a train carrying about 4,000 prisoners to nearby Belsen. The attack caused hundreds of casualties, but many of the prisoners managed to escape into the nearby woods. where several hundred were killed.

Not only were they unaware of the Allied strike on the train of prisoners and the subsequent escape and killing of some, they were not told that it had been only seven or eight months since British and Canadian troops had liberated the concentration camp. This historic event took place on April 15, 1945, just days after the train bombing.

Richard Dimbly, the renowned BBC journalist and broadcaster, was with the liberating troops that day and produced a devastating radio report. His description of what the liberators found is too graphic to recount on these pages, but is dramatically illustrated by the last words of his broadcast: "This was the most horrible day in my life."

Charlotte clearly recalls that, before entering Belsen, their bus was suddenly stopped and they were asked to get out to greet children travelling by them in three trucks.

They were astonished to learn that the children were all either orphans or survivors of the concentration camp, on their way to England or other countries where homes had been found for them. The children were in surprisingly good spirits and obviously excited at the thought of once again having a real home in which to live.

While the children spoke many languages, Aunt Mel (Jean Mills) soon discovered one boy of about fifteen who spoke English very well. "He informed us that he was an accordionist but said it didn't work very well, but he expected to get a really good one when he reached his sister in Atlantic city. We introduced him to Julius Silverman, who we told was a violinist. The boy was a little puzzled because Julius had long hair and a flowing silk tie. Julius, laughing, told him he'd attend to these little matters when he got back to Canada."

After a brief visit with the children, the group moved on to Belsen, where all the buildings had been totally destroyed but for those in a very small open area where they were told 60,000 people had been forced to live in appalling conditions. Nearby, there was a gravesite marked with a sign that read, "2,500 bodies are buried here." They also saw the crematorium where so many bodies had been burned and, standing nearby, the grim outline of what had once been the gallows.

Although it has been more than seventy years since Charlotte witnessed the very disturbing reminders of what Belsen had once been like, she can still vividly recall arriving there. She admits it was overwhelming for her and her concert friends who had been in Canada during the Second World War, to see firsthand such traumatizing evidence of the horrors inflicted on thousands of innocent people during the war.

About a half a mile away from Belsen, they stopped in front of a brightly painted house bearing a sign that identified it as the "Children's House." Inside, they were instantly surrounded by eager, affectionate children who were so obviously starved for affection, they would put their arms around anyone they could—which made it too emotionally painful to try to pull away. What especially shocked the Halifax Heralds was discovering that many of these Jewish children had known nothing but life in the concentration camp. Even worse, the youngsters showed them the numbers tattooed on their arms and told them of having to give their blood for German soldiers.

The group decided they should give an impromptu show for the children and, before they left, gave them all the chocolate they had, which, they agreed, was "painfully inadequate."

After this heart wrenching visit, their guide took them to a hospital on the same grounds. Inside they found hundreds of displaced people in varying states of health who, at last, were being well cared for and nursed back to health. All of those who were well enough to gather in a large hall were treated to a special concert.

Charlotte says she will never forget listening to Julius Silverman playing a selection of traditional Jewish music on his violin for these people. She is wistful as she recalls, "Everyone was teary eyed and very emotional." This day would remain one of most emotional experiences of the Halifax Heralds' tour of Europe.

CHAPTER THIRTEEN
THE LAST LEG OF THE OVERSEAS TOUR

After their visit to Belsen, the Halifax Heralds remained in Germany for another week before returning to Holland. They spent the week of November 5 at the Grand Theatre, Hilversum, where the Dutch people and Canadian service personnel again eagerly received them.

By then they had travelled more than 6,000 miles through Belgium, the Netherlands and Germany. Their official tour ended with a performance at the Canadian General Hospital, Nijmegan, Holland, on November 17, 1945.

The next day, the group traveled to Ostend, Belgium, where they would be boarding a ship to sail across the channel to England. In Ostend, they found hundreds of soldiers also waiting to be transported to England. Unfortunately, fog suddenly engulfed the port in Ostend resulting in a three-day delay, and the Halifax Heralds were once again asked to entertain their bored companions.

In anticipation of returning to Canada, the group had already packed all of their costumes in trunks, which were placed inside the trucks that had followed them during their overseas tour. The only possessions they had left were their basic essentials, which they had carried in two cumbersome army duffel bags during the last five months.

They hadn't expected to be doing any entertaining in full "battle dress." As Jean Mills reported, "Naturally, wearing uniforms and heavy boots didn't allow them to do any dancing, but they were good sports and did their best to entertain the soldiers, who they knew really deserved some musical entertainment." She added, "This is the first time they were billed as 'The Halifax Heralds in Battle Dress!'"

After this unexpected performance, the group was treated to a pleasant surprise. They were informed they would get their wish to visit France. It wasn't going to be to Paris as they had hoped, but they were nonetheless delighted by the opportunity to go to the little town of Lille, in northern France near the border with Belgium.

Although Lille had been invaded by the Germans during the war, it somehow had consumer items the group hadn't seen in months. It was hard for them to believe they were, at last, in a city where the hostilities hadn't left their mark quite so indelibly. Never before had they seen such a display of perfume, which they described as bearing "labels which were the brands of perfume dear to every woman's heart."

None of the women had enough money to buy any of the expensive perfumes, but they all agreed they had loved the chance to do something they hadn't been able to enjoy for a long time—window-shopping!

They gave their last performance in Europe at the dockside in Ostend, to an appreciative audience who learned firsthand how these volunteers from Canada had earned their rave reviews.

Today, Charlotte especially enjoys sharing a letter from a private to the Halifax newspaper, expressing his enthusiastic praise for the entertainment the Halifax Concert Party provided on its tour of Europe. As his letter read, "I am a good old Halifax boy and last night I saw the best show I have ever seen. It went over in such a big way that they wanted more, there is no other show that will come up to it. We fellows over here that have been around England and in Europe we were very lucky to see them. It made us all feel back home last night and, boy, was I happy. Honest, it still thrills me, I can't get over it."

This is just one example of the gratitude the Halifax Heralds received. Not only had these humble performers from Halifax brought music, dancing and laughter to thousands of Canadian military and their allies in Europe, they had also shared their warmth and friendship with countless men, women and children who had somehow managed to survive the destructive forces of war.

In early December 1945, the Mills, nine women members of the Halifax Heralds, and Julius Silverman finally boarded the Queen Elizabeth to sail to New York. Charlotte, however, wouldn't be with the Halifax Heralds on their voyage back to North America. Instead, she would be staying in England for about a month at the Grange residence, run by the Canadian Legion in Aldershot. She did this in advance of an important visit she would soon be paying to an English hospital and a famous surgeon.

While she waited for what would turn out to be a fateful meeting, Charlotte received a surprise request from the Canadian Legion to lay a wreath at the Brookwood Cemetery in Brookwood, Surrey, England. This is the largest cemetery in the United Kingdom and Western Europe. In it is a particularly large Canadian section that honors 199 Canadian servicemen and includes the graves of forty-three men who died of wounds following the Dieppe Raid in August 1942.

Charlotte, who was proudly wearing her dress uniform, says, "I couldn't help but feel it was a great honour to represent Canada."

CHAPTER FOURTEEN
IN THE HANDS OF A MASTER SURGEON

It was because of Hugh Mills' sister, Gertrude, that Charlotte did not return home to Canada with her fellow performers.

Always searching for medical or surgical interventions to help minimize Charlotte's facial anomalies, Gertrude had happened upon an article in a *Reader's Digest* magazine about one Mr. Archibald McIndoe, a skilled plastic surgeon who was operating on wounded servicemen's faces. (It is important here to again explain that in England and Ireland, surgeons are referred to as "Mister " not "Doctor").

Coincidently, this was a much more recent issue of the same magazine in which Charlotte had learned of the makeup that helped conceal port wine stain.

Originally from New Zealand, Archibald McIndoe had advanced his surgical knowledge and skills at the Mayo Clinic in the United States before moving England in 1930. In 1938, he was appointed a consultant plastic surgeon to the Royal Air Force. A year later, following the outbreak of the war, he elected to practice at the Queen Victoria Hospital in East Grinstead. He soon became famous for performing almost-miraculous plastic surgeries on aircrew from many countries who had experienced disfiguring injuries and burns to their faces and bodies.

The British airmen sustained such severe injuries due to the large quantities of highly flammable aviation fuel required to power the Hurricane and Spitfire fighter planes they flew. When hit or crashed, these aircraft exploded into scorching fireballs, creating horrific burns that became known as "Hurricane burns."

According to his biographer Leonard Mosley, McIndoe performed more than 4,500 operations at East Grinstead. He was surgically creating new noses, new eyelids, new ears—and, often, new faces for brutally scarred young men who had lost their own. He once performed thirty-eight operations—which involved meticulously stitching on postage-stamp-sized grafts of skin—on the fingers a young fighter pilot whose hands had been burnt into a solid mass by fire. Remarkably, after spending months in the hospital this traumatized patient regained limited use of his hands. After reading about McIndoe, Gertrude decided to write to him to describe Charlotte's birth defect. Apparently, she did this soon after she knew that Charlotte would be joining the members of Halifax Concert Party Guild and going overseas.

No copies of Gertrude's correspondence still exist, but she must have asked him if he would see Charlotte at his hospital in East Grinstead. She must also have informed the doctor that his medical fees would be covered—with permission from Hugh Mills, who shared her concern about Charlotte's facial anomalies. To this day, Charlotte will tell you that she never received a bill for her surgical care at McIndoe's hospital and the issue of payment was never discussed with her.

Charlotte well remembers the day Gertrude told her the startling news that a famous plastic surgeon had agreed to see her at his hospital in England and that he wanted pictures sent to him.

"Gertrude arranged to have a photographer meet me one night at Mills," Charlotte recalls. "After the store was closed, he took a number of pictures of the right side of my face. I never saw them after they were developed, or before they were sent to Mr. McIndoe."

Not long after the Halifax Heralds had arrived in England, the Mills and Charlotte went by train to see McIndoe at the Queen Victoria Hospital in East Grinstead.

"He was operating and we were taken to the gardens around the hospital to wait for him. When he later met us in his office, I remember him being a very friendly man," Charlotte says. "I later learned that he was a doctor who took a very personal interest in his severely burned patients and that this included recognizing that they also needed lots of emotional support. That day, I remember feeling really assured when he promised me he would see me at his hospital soon after our tour was over."

As it turned out, thanks to the army's ongoing support and the personnel who drove her there, Charlotte would arrive in East Grinstead on January 2, 1946. "I was supposed to be there on New Year's day but it had been too foggy to drive there. The day I arrived I was dressed in my uniform because I didn't have much civilian clothing with me. A nurse admitted me to a large hut-like building where I was given a bed in a large ward. There were six beds on one side and six on the other side and a pot belly stove in the middle of the room—obviously the main source of heat. I learned the other patients were mostly all civilians who had experienced serious injuries—often because of air raids."

She was almost immediately impressed with the head nurse, Miss Leathers, who was very strict but well respected, and who made sure her patients received excellent care.

Charlotte still has copies of the medical records written during her six-month stay at the Queen Elizabeth Hospital. They record a period in her life that most people might have found unbearable, but she expresses only gratitude and impressive pragmatism regarding the often-painful procedures she endured.

Mr McIndoe outside an operating room at the Canadian wing of the Queen Victoria Hospital. Charlotte took the picture.

The day she was admitted, her medical chart indicates that she was in good overall health and that the congenital cavernous haemangioma (commonly known as a port wine stain) on the right side of her face had not increased in size. However, the chart states that the haemangioma had broken down and bled a number of times during the previous two or three years. This affected almost all of the right side of her face. It extended to the right half of her upper lip, which was thickened, and to the inners side of the lip and the mucous membrane of her gums. And there was an associated anomaly- a large polyp obstructed most of the tip of her nose. The chart also stated that she had never had any surgical treatment.

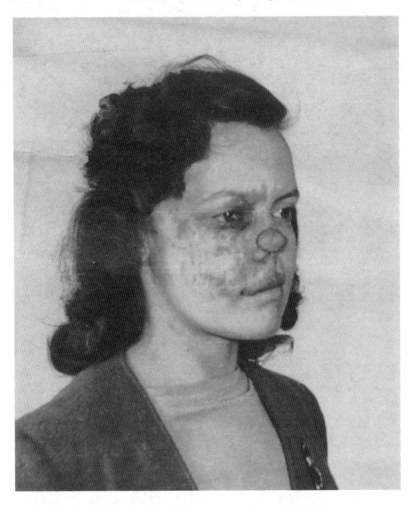

Without any make up before she had surgery in 1946 Mr. McIndoe had drawn a mark around the nose where he would be performing plastic surgery.

Nine days after this assessment, Charlotte underwent her first operation. Five more would follow over the next six months, which would involve complex and difficult plastic and dental surgery.

Charlotte still has all of McIndoe's operating notes in her personal medical record. Even a layperson without any surgical knowledge, would have recognized that the procedures must have been very complex and painful.

The first operation was a dental procedure, which involved extracting two molars and some of her jaw.

The next procedure was far more invasive. First, McIndoe excised the skin from around her nose that had been covered by a port wine stain. Then, using a skin graft from her right forehead, he turned down a flap, medically known as a pedicle. Next, he sewed the pedicle, which still contained a blood supply, into place on the area of her nose that no longer had skin covering it. He also took a skin graft from her right thigh to cover the excised area on her forehead.

The results of this procedure were startling. In Charlotte's case, it left her with a strange elephant-like trunk of healthy skin still attached to her forehead and covering the middle of her face. The ungainly skin remained there for about three weeks.

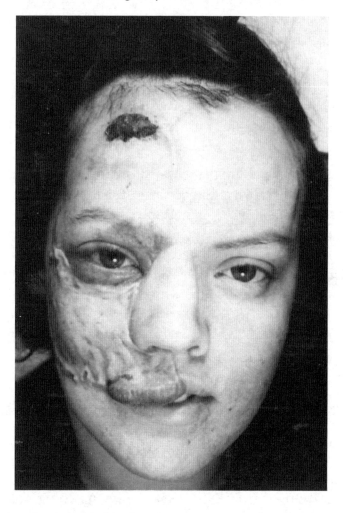

Charlotte's face after she had had her first plastic surgery – showing where the graft was taken

There were complications from this surgery. It turned out that the skin graft from her forehead had been cut too deeply.

Charlotte is forthcoming about what happened as a result of this re-grafting procedure. "They had a terrible time getting the first bandage covering my forehead off. It just wouldn't come off and several doctors and a few nurses each attempted to remove it. It finally was removed but I have to admit, it was very painful and I thought I was going to faint."

The next surgery involved removing the skin flap that had been excised from Charlotte's forehead and then suturing a grafted piece of skin permanently in place over her nose.

A fourth operation, performed in March, 1946, was necessary because of the x-ray treatments she had received in Halifax when she was a little girl. As she already knew, this treatment had exacerbated her facial problems and actually burnt the skin. This time, McIndoe excised the burned area and covered it with another skin graft removed from the inner side of her left thigh.

Following skin-grafting surgery, Charlotte would usually have to stay in bed for several days and receive intravenous penicillin therapy that she found very unpleasant.

Happily, there was something that cheered her up during those days spent in bed—a record that had arrived at the hospital. "It had taken a long time to get to me because of some complicated circumstances, but when I was able to play it, it was really hilarious," recounts Charlotte. "I learned it had been recorded at the CBC in Halifax. A lot of the people who had been with me during our tour overseas were heard on it. They took turns singing, telling jokes or just sending me their best wishes." She still has the antiquated recording and, every so often, listens to it on a very old record player.

After two more operations and several additional procedures, Charlotte sensed her stay at the Queen Victoria Hospital was coming to an end, and she was right.

Looking back at all she had gone through, one can't help asking her about the moments in her six-month stay at the hospital when she must have felt very frightened, or at great risk.

"Well, there certainly was one day I'll never forget! It happened in March, 1946, when the house doctor came to see me and told me they needed my bed and I would have to leave the hospital. This was terribly upsetting because I was still scheduled for more surgery and, after all, unlike the other patients, I didn't have a home to go to."

Very apprehensive, she immediately sent a telegram to Hugh Mills telling him about the alarming news she had received.

She soon received two telegrams from Halifax. The first came from the Mills. It read: "Charlotte dear, everything under perfect control. Please take our word for it. Writing full details today. Do nothing without McIndoe's advice. Love Uncle, Auntie and Gert."

The other telegram came from her father and read: "You did the right thing. No need financial worry. Uncle calling you. Follow Mr. Mac's advice. Love Dad."

Apparently, the cable from the Mills quickly put the issue of her having to leave the hospital to rest. It was never mentioned again. Although this was a stressful episode, Charlotte had many enjoyable times at East Grinstead and smiles when she reflects upon them.

One memory she loves to talk about is watching nurses using dry tea leaves to sweep the floor in her ward. She also likes to recall the days when she was able to walk and was given the duty, around six o'clock in the morning, to push around a breakfast cart containing tea and toast to the patients on her ward who were still in bed.

Another episode occurred when she took a patient, who was herself a surgeon, to a viewing area over an operating room to watch a surgery being performed on another patient's nose. It seems this doctor was scheduled to have plastic surgery performed on her hands and must have wanted a close-up view of the skills of the surgeon who would be doing her own operation.

Charlotte laughs when she recalls that the free cigarettes she received every month from the army earned her considerable brownie points among many of the other patients. "I gave most of them away, especially to a English wren who was given a bed next to mine. She had fallen off a horse and had been at East Grinstead before. Because she was rather snobby, she wasn't at all liked. I didn't know anything about her and we got along very well and, of course, the free cigarettes helped sustain our friendship. Later, I received a letter from another patient who thanked me for the free chocolates, tin peaches and cigarettes I had given her."

She chuckles a little when she discloses that, at the time, she was the only Canadian still in the hospital and one patient often referred to her as "Miss Canada."

On two pleasant occasions, she was invited to join some of the male patients to attend hockey matches in London. "It was in April, 1946, when I went with them by bus to the Empire Pool Club in Wimbly. We were there to watch a Canadian hockey team play, and if my memory serves, the other team was from Czechoslovakia."

CHAPTER FIFTEEN
MCINDOE AND HIS AMAZING GUINEA PIGS

Above all, Charlotte will never forget playing the only piano in the hospital's Canadian wing: "All of the Canadian patients had been discharged, but I did play for airmen from a number of countries." Perhaps, because of her own pronounced awareness of how people react to significant facial anomalies, she never refers to how any of them looked.

Yet, without question, some of them had faces that were quite grotesque. In Leonard Mosley's biography of Archibald McIndoe entitled, *Faces from the Fire*, he writes about their almost monstrous images: "In every bed lay a shape which had once been a young man, some with a nose hanging down in front of his ravaged face like an elephant trunk, another staring through watering, lidless eyes. There were the jawless and the nose less and the ones with holes in their heads through which the bones protruded."

But as Charlotte will tell you, her surgeon insisted that the wards provide these men with an uplifting environment. He wanted cheerful music, fresh flowers (changed every day) placed beside every man's table, and old hospital mattresses replaced with comfortable new ones. He arranged to have barrels of beer on the wards to encourage an informal and happy atmosphere. Though it might raise eyebrows nowadays, it is also reported that McIndoe liked to have good-looking nurses on his hospital staff. And a nurse wouldn't last long unless she was cheerful and "human," as well as efficient and attractive.

McIndoe was adamant that his seriously disfigured patients not become reclusive, and insisted they visit places such as the pubs in East Grinstead. He also convinced the local families in the town to accept his patients as guests and the other residents to treat them as normally as possible. East Grinstead became known as "the town that did not stare."

Some of the pub owners had taken down the mirrors in their establishments because they felt it would make it easier for the disfigured men who visited there. However, one of those severely injured men had responded to this decision by advising a pub owner to: "Put the mirrors back. We can stand the sight of our faces as long as you don't mind."

Today, almost seventy-five years after her stay at the Queen Victoria Hospital, Charlotte has a collection of newspaper articles about the Guinea Pig Club, formed in 1941 by patients of "Archie" McIndoe, as he was often known. Choosing this name for their club couldn't have been more appropriate because, before his time, treatment of burns was in its infancy. Before his medical and surgical innovations, severely burned causalities had often not survived. But, thanks to McIndoe's advances—which were often experimental in nature—most of his patients survived and some of them even returned to military service.

Mr. McIndoe in his hospital sitting next to man playing the piano. He is surrounded by a few "guinea pigs," nurses and some staff members

In order to belong to the Guinea Pig Club, members had to be serving airmen who had gone through at least ten surgical procedures. Included in the exclusive club's membership were the surgeons and anesthetists who had treated them. By the end of the war, the club had 649 members from fourteen countries, including a number of Canadians (57% were British; 27% were Canadian; 8% were New Zealanders; 8% were Australian). At the end of the war, of the 649 Guinea Pigs, 176 were Canadians.

One of the "renowned" Canadian Guinea Pigs was Norm McHolm from Goderick, Ontario. He had been a flight lieutenant in the Canadian Air Force during the Second World War and had had a terrible plane crash in England. He had experienced awful injuries; his rescuers found his nose in his oxygen mask and handed it to a doctor." But, thanks to various operations involving skin grafts, skillful incisions and remedial plastic surgery performed at the hospital in East Grimstead, he went on to fly more bombing missions over Germany.

Charlotte never mentions it but she, no doubt, was a positive ally for these men, who also had to learn to deal with the complex anguish of living in a body others may have found repugnant.

In his biography of Archibald McIndoe, Leonard Mosley writes that not only was he a plastic surgeon with no equals, he was also a man who believed his mutilated young patients required more than surgery. McIndoe insisted that they also needed mental and emotional support. To provide this, he fostered a relationship between himself and his patients that "would clean the wounds from the mind as well as the body." That is why his "guinea pig patients" truly venerated him, as Charlotte still does.

CHAPTER SIXTEEN
RETURNING HOME

Charlotte will never forget the day Mr. McIndoe informed her that he felt it was time for her to leave the Queen Victoria Hospital. "He explained that he had performed all the surgery I could have for now and that I would need time to allow healing to take place before having more done," she recounts. "He told me that I had two options to consider—to go to a private clinic he owned to wait for more surgery, or go home to Canada and when it came time to have more plastic surgery, arrange to see Dr. Ross Tilley in Toronto. I was aware that during the war, this Canadian surgeon had worked at the Queen Victoria Hospital with McIndoe and had the reputation of also being another excellent plastic surgeon. By now, I had great faith in Mr. McIndoe, so I decided to go home and follow his advice."

Soon after, Charlotte returned to the Grange Hotel in Aldershot run by the Canadians. A few weeks later she began her ocean voyage back to Canada.

She admits that she has few memories of that voyage, except for one evening having dinner at the captain's table. She still remembers her ship, the *Aquitania*, docking at a pier in Halifax on July 29, 1946. She clearly enjoys describing that moment when she walked down the gangplank in her dress uniform, excited about having a pair of high heeled shoes on her feet. She knew this daring act would amuse those who were waiting for her. "Waiting for me at the dock was Uncle Mel and all of the members of the Halifax Herald group who had been with me during our six-month tour overseas!"

The late Irene Cowieson (Spence), who had been one of Charlotte's closest friends, was among the people waiting to welcome Charlotte home. Years later, she remembered that day very well. She was somewhat tentative when, before her death, she was asked how Charlotte looked, but she did say, "Candidly, we had all hoped she would come back looking like a movie star. Of course, that hadn't happened, but her appearance had certainly been very much improved."

CHAPTER SEVENTEEN
SETTLING INTO POSTWAR LIFE

When asked how her friends and family reacted to her improved appearance, Charlotte insists no one mentioned it: "I suppose they were uncomfortable commenting, and you know it was a time when people just avoided saying things that were unkind."

She went back to the apartment at the Waegwoltic Club, where her father, stepmother and two half-brothers lived. "I also went back to Mills Brothers, which was pleasant because everyone seemed pleased to have me back. Once again, besides serving customers, I focused on displays and the front windows. I also enjoyed once again being one of the store's buyers. This required me to visit a number of hotels in the city to see merchandise being offered by representatives of companies that manufactured things such as coats, dresses, purses, etc. we sold at Mills Brothers."

Something else happened soon after she arrived back in Nova Scotia that proved to be a most unusual experience for Charlotte. She can't recall exactly when it happened, but she has a newspaper clipping taken from a Halifax newspaper and has learned the same story also appeared in the *Chicago Tribune*.

This experience came about because of Brett Fader, a man who had travelled with the Halifax Heralds overseas. After returning to Nova Scotia, he had become an amateur radio operator. Almost every day, he would sit at his radio contacting other so-called "ham operators" around the world.

One of the operators he reached was on an American weather station located close to the north pole. One day this fellow was chatting with Fader from his floating ice island, when, obviously feeling a little blue, he told Fader how much he and his friends missed girls and declared, "Oh, to hear a female voice!"

Fader immediately thought of Charlotte and arranged for her to have a "chat with them." Apparently, the men were overjoyed to hear her voice and later said she did much to maintain morale on the lonely ice island.

Soon after this delightful experience, Charlotte decided to follow McIndoe's advice. She contacted Dr. Ross Tilley in Toronto to arrange to have him perform any plastic surgery he felt was necessary.

She knew that Dr. Tilley had spent time with Archibald McIndoe at his hospital in East Grimstead and that he was one of Canada's top plastic surgeons with an impressive reputation. In fact, she had learned that, due to the increased number of Canadian casualties, a Canadian wing was built at East Grinstead and Dr. Tilley was one of the leaders planning it. In 1944, he was made an Officer of the Order of the British Empire for his leadership in pioneering new techniques for treating burns.

Her high expectations of Dr. Tilley were validated after she paid him several visits in Toronto which, in all cases, included him performing plastic surgery on her.

Understandably, this happened a long time ago, so she can no longer remember many of the details. She does, however, have copies of letters she received from him. One was dated September 18, 1948. It reads: "Enclosed please find the photographs I promised to send on. They turned out reasonably well."

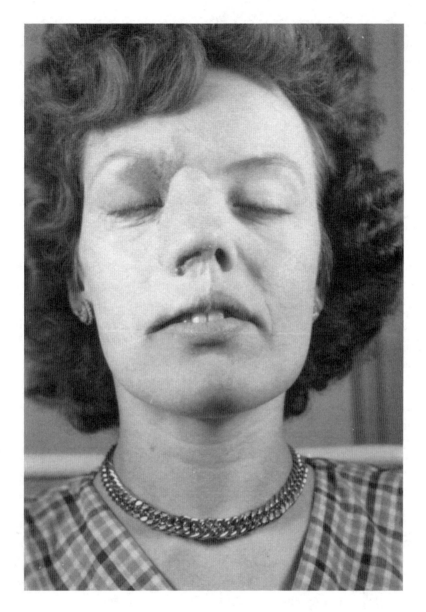

Charlotte's face is obviously very much improved.

He adds: "Too bad your friend did not make out more successfully in the American competition, however, she certainly did well at home." He was referring to Betty Jean Ferguson, Charlotte's good friend who had appeared with her during the Halifax Herald's concert party tours in Halifax and who had won the Miss Canada pageant in 1948. She, however, hadn't done well in the Miss America pageant the same year.

Charlotte also has a letter from Dr. Tilly dated October 24, 1955. In this correspondence he writes, "I think it is possible that the appearance of the nose might be improved by putting in some cartilage support, this should help keep the nostril open and at the same time, we could see what is going on inside the nose. If you decide to come to Toronto, please let me know five weeks ahead, so that I can arrange hospital accommodation for you. Am glad to hear of your continuing interest in the entertainment field."

Charlotte, along with Lila, had continued to perform at many musical events. "We appeared at many conventions, social functions and lots of other events."

Later, while in New York on a buying trip for Mills Brothers, she learned Jean Mills had died. "I was sad because I had always truly admired her."

Not long after this distressing loss, it was necessary for Hugh Mills to go overseas once again to visit fashionable businesses in London and in countries such as Germany, France, Italy and the Netherlands. In 1960, he took Charlotte and his sister Gertrude with him. Charlotte has lovely memories of that trip, which included visits to small villages where local artisans set up displays of their exquisite handicrafts. "One day, in a French village, we sat with the workers, ate lunch with them at a large table and really enjoyed being part of such a unique environment. I had learned French—from grade three to high school—so I was able to talk a little with the people."

The trip was saddened, however, because while they were in Florence, Charlotte received a telegram telling her that her father had suffered a stroke and died on March 29, 1960.

During the same 1960 visit to Europe, she was pleased to once again have met Mr. McIndoe—only by this time he was Sir Archibald McIndoe. The good surgeon had been knighted by the queen in 1947 for his outstanding efforts, not only to repair the faces and bodies of the young men so tragically burned in World War Two, but to restore their spirits as well.

Ironically, and sadly, his death occurred only about two weeks after her father's death, which had happened on April 12, 1960. The great innovator and healer had died in his sleep of a heart attack at the age of 59. His legacy lives on, however, through the Blond McIndoe Research Foundation, which conducts research to advance the science of wound healing, and the McIndoe Burns Unit at the Queen Victoria Hospital in East Grinstead, where burn victims continue to receive the best available care.

In 2014, a bronze statue of him caring for an injured RCAF pilot was unveiled by Princess Anne in East Grinstead, which is not far from the Queen Victoria Hospital where he had performed his amazing surgery.

CHAPTER EIGHTEEN
A DRAMATIC CHANGE IN CHARLOTTE'S LIFE

Charlotte experienced a dramatic personal transition in the late 1950s, when a gentleman named Don Jeffries came into her life. By then, she had been living for four years in an apartment over Mills Brothers.

Don Jeffries had opened the Four Corners Gallery across the street from Mills and often saw Charlotte arranging its front windows. One day, he came over to the store and introduced himself to Hugh Mills. While there, he happened to stop and speak with Charlotte.

Soon, they began seeing each other. "We would go on picnics together and I remember going with him to a Halifax Symphony Ball, and we also often went dancing because he was a wonderful dancer!"

Charlotte going to Halifax Symphony Ball with Don. Painting hanging behind her on the wall is one she had done while she was in high school.

It was about two years later that he invited her to dinner at his home on Purcell's Cove Road. "He had bought the house about a year or so before and because it didn't have any landscaping, he was spending lot of time on the outside property," says Charlotte. "It was his birthday and I knew he was doing so much hard work around the place, so I arranged to have a fertilizer spreader delivered to his address. Of course, I certainly didn't know that he had bought me a diamond engagement ring, but it seems the two women who were salesladies at his store were really excited about what they knew was going to happen that night. I'm sure they must have really laughed when they learned that I had received my engagement ring and had given him only a fertilizer spreader!"

On May 12, 1962, Don and Charlotte were married at St. Paul's Church in Halifax. She was forty years old and he was forty-seven. In the description of their wedding, which appeared in the *Halifax Herald*, it was noted that, for many years, she had been employed by Mills Brothers and "is well known in the musical and entertainment field." Her husband was described as a graduate of teacher's college in Fredericton and Columbia University, a former professor of art education at the Nova Scotia College of Art, and current owner of the Four Corners Gallery Limited. The article did not include something that Charlotte has always been proud of—that Don had served on the staff of the Canadian consul-general in New York for several years.

Don and Charlotte coming out of church the day they were married.

Charlotte feels it is important to disclose that, because of her age and concerns that any child she would bear might have serious facial anomalies, she and Don never contemplated having children.

Not long before their wedding, Charlotte decided to stay at home. She left Mills and began focusing most of her time and attention on the property around her new home on Purcell's Cove Road: "He had overplanted it and I had to keep pruning it."

The joy of gardening soon became—and continues to be—one of the most fulfilling aspects of her life. Over the years, Charlotte has filled her surroundings with a profusion of magnificent plants and flowers. After her marriage, she also continued to accept musical performance opportunities but, since her friend Lila had moved away, she presented only piano recitals.

Don became quite ill in the late 1960s. Because of his serious breathing problems, he couldn't spend long hours at the Four Corners Gallery anymore. Charlotte realized she had no choice but to fill his role at the store.

Joan Doherty, who now owns the very popular Marigold Bed and Breakfast Inn in west-end Halifax, is one of Charlotte's closest friends. She, no doubt, has the most vivid memories of the time when Charlotte had to assume managing their store on Spring Garden Road.

As fate would have it, Joan was only eighteen years old and a new graduate of the Sacred Heart Convent in Halifax when she first met Charlotte. "I had always loved making creative things such as pretty handmade cloth dolls, and had brought two of them to the Four Corners Gallery, hoping they might agree to sell them. One was kind of folksy, the other very traditional and when Charlotte saw them, she liked them very much and called her husband to see if he thought they should do this. He agreed and soon they were in the gallery's windows and I was so pleased when my dolls became very popular with passersby."

Joan was delighted when Charlotte offered her a room over the gallery to create her dolls, which soon became bestsellers. Charlotte also hired her to be a sales clerk at the gallery during the summer months that followed. She admired Charlotte's competent running of the store which, combined with her sense of fun and interest in everyone, made the shop a place that staff and customers enjoyed all year round. The merchandise and displays changed with the seasons and attracted a varied clientele who were treated like friends. "It was a very happy place and I never thought running the store might be too challenging for her."

She becomes somber when she remembers coming into the store one morning to learn that Don Jeffries had died suddenly the night before.

Charlotte will certainly never forget that heartbreaking episode: "I had been at the hospital having some minor plastic surgery performed by Dr. James Ross and had been discharged. Don was supposed to pick me up but, when he never arrived, I took a taxi home and to my great distress, found him lying on the bedroom floor. I called a neighbour who was a doctor and he called an ambulance, but Don never survived."

It was only about two years after his death in 1971, that Charlotte stopped renting the space for the Four Corners Gallery, "Don had always advised me that if he could no longer run the store, I shouldn't try to do this. And he was right."

Joan recalls Charlotte telling her that, after working in the retail business for so many years, she felt it was time to retire. Joan, however, emphasizes, "We have been friends now for more than forty-five years, but every time I'm with her, she's never changed. For me, she's exactly the same lady I first knew so long ago!"

CHAPTER NINETEEN
CHARLOTTE PREDICTABLY REMAINS A REMARKABLE WOMAN

The years following her husband's death have again demonstrated Charlotte's ability to cope well with the challenges of human existence. She never went back to work, but instead, concentrated on her love of gardening and enjoying a convivial group of friends. And she continued playing the piano almost daily, something she had been doing since her early childhood. This latter achievement has been personally rewarding for her, because she is aware that her lovely playing has enhanced the lives of many other people.

Charlotte enjoys talking about another, somewhat surprising, activity she started in the early 1980s. She insists she wants to share this time in her life so people will know that she took pleasure in a pastime that had nothing to do with music! "This happened when an old friend of mine, Walter Purcell, who had been our plumber and who became a good friend, invited me to go fishing with him and his wife Sheelagh on the North West Arm. He had a dock on it which was across the street from his home on Purcell's Cove Road. He also invited my neighbour Ron Horrocks, who was Halifax's fire chief, and his wife Marina, to come along."

Charlotte found fishing so enjoyable, it soon became a regular activity. "We'd get up, usually on the weekend around six a.m. (and sometimes in the evenings), and go to Walter's dock and climb onto his boat. Often during the daytime, we would stay out for five or six hours and anchor somewhere in Halifax Harbour. I turned out to be a very good fisherman and usually caught a lot of mackerel, cod and occasionally, haddock. I became quite proud of myself when I learned how to clean and fillet fish and, best of all, how to skillfully pick the worms out of the cod!"

Charlotte is particularly pleased to share a letter she received dated June 19, 1979, from the Marine Fish Division in Dartmouth. The letter thanked her for returning a tag from a codfish she had caught and informed her that the cod had been tagged in Halifax Harbour by members of its staff on February, 28, 1979. She was also intrigued to learn that, although the fish had been injected with the antibiotic tetracycline, it was still safe to eat.

Charlotte says someone did eat that tagged codfish, but she was amused to learn that if she had sent the fish—frozen, along with its tag—to the Marine Fish Division, she would have received $5.00 plus a dollar for every pound it weighed! Instead, her reward for returning only its tag was a check for $3.00.

Charlotte's days of fishing are over now that she is in her nineties, but she has never stopped playing music, often at a nursing home not far from where she lives. She is well aware that the residents truly enjoy her piano renditions and that many become quite nostalgic when she plays songs or music they used to hear many years ago.

When asked about the people who have had the greatest impact on her life, Charlotte immediately speaks of the plastic surgeons whose skillful hands had done their best to change the aggressive lesions on her face.

Charlotte still treasures two letters that her English plastic surgeon had written to her after she returned to Nova Scotia. One of them, dated, November 7, 1946, says, "I am delighted to hear that your face has settled down. Of course, there will be edges and rough patches for some considerable time yet. Perhaps, when you are a year or two older, you will save up and come over to England and let me do what final trimming is necessary. In any case, it is grand to know you are back home and on top of the world. I would very much like to get a photograph showing your present condition."

He had also thanked her for some nylons she had sent to him: "Yes, the nylons did arrive and were greeted with excitement and enthusiasm. They are decorating the right pairs of legs and I understand have already caused great trouble where they have been exhibited."

The other letter from him was dated February 19, 1947: "I was delighted to receive pictures of your face, which showed a very marked improvement on those taken here before you left... It will take a long time before all the little dents disappear from your face and it might be that there are one or two areas in which something further might be done if they do not settle down. Nevertheless, you will always have to use some foundation cream to make it blend up with the rest." And he added, "We are all very busy here and miss your cheery presence. I will look forward to hearing from you from time to time."

Another doctor of whom she speaks highly of is Dr. James Ross, a Halifax plastic surgeon. Dr. Tilley had advised her to see him because this meant she would not have to travel so often to Toronto. She saw Dr. Ross quite often during the 1950s.

I think I should share with you the fact that I had once worked with him. This happened while I was a registered nurse at the IWK Hospital for Children in Halifax. In the early 1980's, while I was a reporter with CBC television, he played a significant role in a prize- winning documentary I had hosted. It was a sensitive account of several of his seriously burned patients, and it won an international film award.He is now in his nineties, and I was delighted to reach him at his home in rural Nova Scotia. He made it clear that he had only done minor procedures on Charlotte but said that he had always admired her and that she had become a special friend.

Another plastic surgeon who did perform major surgery on her face was Dr. Oleh Antonyshyn. This happened in 1990 at the Victoria General Hospital in Halifax. His operative report indicates that he had performed extensive plastic surgery on her right upper lip to correct a progressive deformity.

Since then, Charlotte has been to see three other plastic surgeons. The late Dr. M. Caines saw her only once, but did not perform any surgery on her. But, he did comment, "She really is a fascinating case. I think she is the first person I have seen who was operated on by the legendary McIndoe."

Dr. Winston Parkhill saw her several times between 1992 and 2001. The only medical information on record says he performed minor procedures on her lip and nose.

At present, she is seeing Dr. Jason Williams, a Halifax plastic surgeon. She discloses that, because she is now well over ninety, they agreed it would be unwise to subject her to more surgery. He did, however, remove a small cancerous area near one of her eyes. Obviously, having Charlotte for a patient was memorable for him, as he declared "Charlotte is a living piece of plastic surgical history. Her experiences with both Sir Archibald McInroe and Dr. Ross Tilley, both pioneers in our specialty, are unique and very special."

EPILOGUE

Charlotte, at ninety-five, continues to live on her own. She is pragmatic about her future, but insists that participating in Tai Chi for more than fifteen years has helped keep her physically active. She also is convinced that she wouldn't be able to remain in her own home without significant support from a number of people. While she regrets that her two older brothers, Ross and Tom, died long ago, she is grateful that her two half brothers, George and Roger Guy, visit her frequently and offer lots of encouragement.

Charlotte says that two neighbours, Angela Sykes and Nick Webb, deserve a medal for their constant assistance: "They have also been true advocates for me. I don't know how I can possibly thank them enough for what they have done for me.

Today - In her greenhouse (credit - Nick Webb)

Apart from her independence, Charlotte has also maintained her sense of humour. But, she still wants to emphasizes that although she has great admiration for the wonderful plastic surgeons who operated on her, it was never possible to stop her skin abnormality from returning.

"Today, a large polyp is again obstructing my left nostril, the right half of my upper lip. The mucous membranes inside my mouth and an area around my left eye now all display the long term effects that the cavernous hemangiomas has had on me.

Nevertheless, despite her serious facial problems, she can still make light of them: "Here I am in my nineties and I still have to get up early every day 'to put my face on' before anyone comes to my front door. And the strange thing about it is, I never look the same two days in a row."

Then she adds mischievously, "The only time I do go out without my makeup on is very early in the morning so I can put my garbage out!"

A significant issue I had to address when I approached Charlotte was her reticence about writing this book about her. She insisted modestly, "I know many people who have had a far more traumatic life than mine."

I wasn't prepared to argue with her, so, in order to receive official confirmation of my belief that she is an extraordinary woman, I turned to her dear friend Budge Wilson, the well – known Canadian writer,

When I told her that Charlotte was insisting that there isn't anything exceptional about her, she took only a few seconds to reply. "In my opinion," she stated emphatically, "Charlotte is a real heroine!"

It has been a true joy and an honour to have had the profound and reflective details of her remarkable life shared with me and to be able to convey her inspiring story to readers who, like me, will be in awe of her inspiring response to the immeasurable challenges she has been given.

Her accordion is still close at hand! (credit Nick Webb)

Printed in Canada